PEYTON MANNING
Football Superstar

BY MIKE ARTELL

CAPSTONE PRESS
a capstone imprint

Sports Illustrated KIDS Superstar Athletes is published by Capstone Press,
151 Good Counsel Drive, P.O. Box 669, Mankato, Minnesota 56002.
www.capstonepub.com

Books published by Capstone Press are manufactured with paper
containing at least 10 percent post-consumer waste.

Library of Congress Cataloging-in-Publication Data
Artell, Mike.
    Peyton Manning : football superstar / by Mike Artell.
        p. cm.—(Sports Illustrated Kids, superstar athletes)
    Includes bibliographical references and index.
    Summary: "Presents the athletic biography of Peyton Manning, including his career as a high school,
college, and professional football player"—Provided by publisher.
    ISBN 978-1-4296-6564-3 (library binding)
    ISBN 978-1-4296-7311-2 (paperback)
    1. Manning, Peyton—Juvenile literature. 2. Football players—United States—Biography—Juvenile
literature. 3. Quarterbacks (Football)—United States—Biography—Juvenile literature.
I. Title.
    GV939.M289A77 2012
    796.332092—dc22
    [B]   2011001020

Editorial Credits
Christopher L. Harbo, editor; Ted Williams, designer; Eric Gohl, media researcher;
    Eric Manske, production specialist

Photo Credits
Newscom/Icon SMI/TSN/Albert Dickson, 13; Robert Seale, 10
Sports Illustrated/Al Tielemans, 7, 22 (top & middle); Bill Frakes, cover (left), 9; Bob Rosato, 1, 5,
    16, 19, 23; Damian Strohmeyer, 15 (back); David E. Klutho, 22 (bottom); John Biever, cover
    (right), 6, 17, 21, 24; John Iacono, 15 (front); Peter Read Miller, 2–3

Design Elements
Shutterstock/chudo-yudo, designerpix, Fassver Anna, Fazakas Mihaly

Direct Quotations
Page 18, from September 3, 2005, *USA Today* article "Colts' Triplets May Be Embarking
    on Swan Song Season" by Mike Chappell, www.usatoday.com
Page 20, from February 4, 2007, *CBS News* article "Colts Conquer at Soggy Super Bowl"
    by James M. Klatell, www.cbsnews.com

Printed in the United States of America in North Mankato, Minnesota.
032011   006110GCF11

TABLE OF CONTENTS

CHAPTER 1

BATTLING THE BEARS

In the 2007 Super Bowl, Peyton Manning and the Indianapolis Colts battled the Chicago Bears. Rain and mud caused players to drop the ball and miss chances to score. Manning slowed the game down. He picked the Bears apart with short passes. At halftime, the Colts were up 16–14.

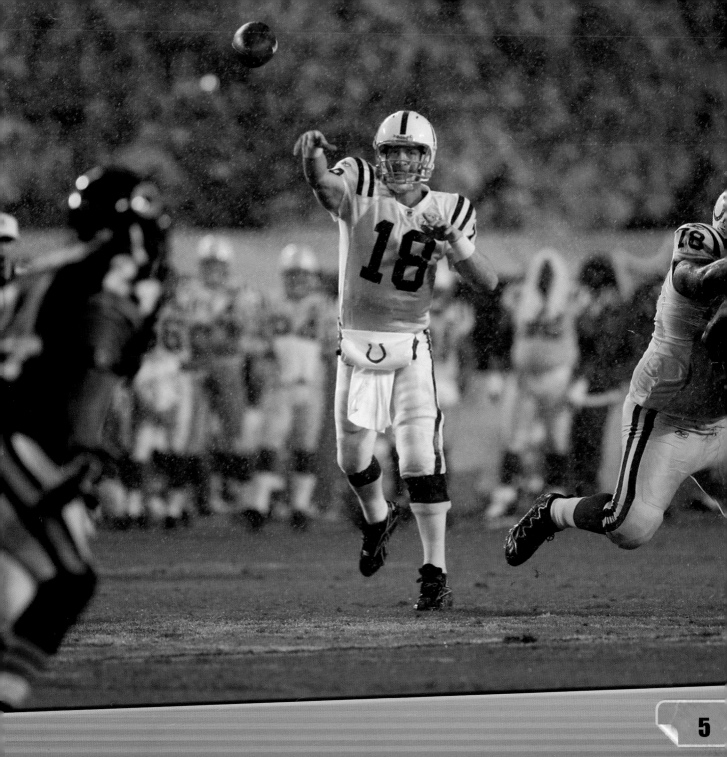

Kelvin Hayden rushes for a touchdown after making an interception.

In the second half, Manning stayed cool and played steady. He led his team to two field goals. The Bears added one. With less than 12 minutes left, the Colts **intercepted** a pass. The team scored a touchdown. Manning and his Colts were Super Bowl champions.

intercept—to catch a pass by the opposing team

CHAPTER 2

RISING STAR

Peyton Williams Manning was born March 24, 1976, in New Orleans, Louisiana. In high school he was the star quarterback for the Isidore Newman Greenies. As a senior he passed for 2,703 yards and 39 touchdowns. Manning won a 1993–1994 National Player of the Year award.

FOOTBALL FAMILY

Football runs in Manning's family. His father, Archie (right), was a quarterback for the New Orleans Saints. His brother Eli (left) plays quarterback for the New York Giants. Eli is also a Super Bowl champion.

Manning played college football for the University of Tennessee Volunteers. In his freshman year, two other Tennessee quarterbacks got hurt. Manning became the starting quarterback. He won seven of the next eight games. He also earned a Freshman of the Year award.

The next year Manning threw 22 touchdown passes. As a junior, he threw for more than 3,000 yards. He also helped Tennessee win the Citrus Bowl. As a senior, Manning was named the nation's top athlete. He was a runner-up for the Heisman Trophy.

amateur—an athlete who is not paid for taking part in a sport

COLLEGE RECORDS

Manning set 33 University of Tennessee records. His records included 11,201 passing yards, 863 pass completions, and 89 touchdown passes.

CHAPTER 3

NFL GLORY

The Indianapolis Colts made Manning the top pick in the 1998 National Football League (NFL) **draft**. As a **rookie**, he broke many of the NFL's first-year passing records. The next year Manning threw for more than 4,000 yards. He played in the Pro Bowl at the end of the season.

draft—the process of choosing a person to join a sports team
rookie—a first-year player

Manning became known for his passing **accuracy**. In his first 12 seasons, he threw a record 366 touchdown passes. He also passed for more than 3,000 yards in each of those years.

accuracy—the ability to hit a set target on the field

In 2003 he threw six touchdowns and only five incomplete passes in a single game. In the 2004 season he threw 49 touchdowns and only 10 interceptions.

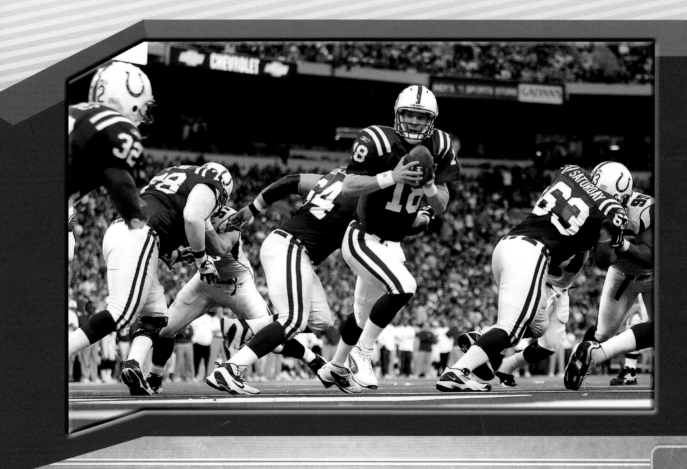

In 2009 Manning and the Colts won 14 straight games. He also became the fourth quarterback to throw for more than 50,000 career yards. At season's end, the Colts fell to the New Orleans Saints in the Super Bowl. Manning was voted Most Valuable Player (MVP) in the NFL for the fourth time.

"I've never taken for granted what we've had, not for one single game, not one single practice. I've truly been blessed."—Peyton Manning

CHAPTER 4

COOL UNDER PRESSURE

Manning is a smart quarterback. He throws the ball quickly and accurately. He is also a **patient** player. He doesn't get worried when his team falls behind. His team and his fans trust him. They know he'll make good decisions on the field.

patient—calm during difficult times

"It's hard to put into words. I'm proud to be part of this team."
—Peyton Manning

TIMELINE

1976—Peyton Manning is born March 24 in New Orleans, Louisiana.

1993—Manning ends his high school football career with 34 wins and five losses as a starting quarterback.

1997—Manning connects on four touchdown passes in the Florida Citrus Bowl; he is the game's MVP.

1998—Indianapolis takes Manning as the first pick in the NFL draft.

1999—Manning leads the Colts to a 13–3 season; he plays in the Pro Bowl at the end of the season.

2007—Manning and the Colts defeat the Chicago Bears in the Super Bowl.

2010—Manning is named the NFL's MVP for a record fourth time.

GLOSSARY

accuracy (AK-yuh-rah-see)—the ability to hit a set target on the field

amateur (A-muh-chuhr)—an athlete who is not paid for taking part in a sport

draft (DRAFT)—the process of choosing a person to join a sports team

intercept (in-tur-SEPT)—to catch a pass by the opposing team

patient (PAY-shunt)—calm during difficult times

rookie (RUK-ee)—a first-year player

READ MORE

Glaser, Jason. *Peyton Manning.* New York: Gareth Stevens Pub., 2011.

Wilner, Barry. *Peyton Manning: a Football Star Who Cares.* Sports Stars Who Care. Berkeley Heights, N.J.: Enslow Publishers, Inc., 2011.

INTERNET SITES

FactHound offers a safe, fun way to find Internet sites related to this book. All of the sites on FactHound have been researched by our staff.

Here's all you do:

Visit *www.facthound.com*

Type in this code: 9781429665643

 Check out projects, games and lots more at
www.capstonekids.com

INDEX